Roman Britain
Resource Book

Contents

Romans and Britons

Rome and its Empire

This is Rome in Italy. The people who lived here in **ancient times** made Rome a great city. You can see the ruins of some of their buildings in this picture.

Ancient times

A very long time ago indeed.

This is a model of what Rome looked like in those days.

The Romans were very good at fighting as well as building. Just over two thousand years ago their armies took over all the other towns and people in Italy.

Then they took over the lands of people living outside Italy.

The land they ruled is called the 'Roman Empire'. You can see it marked on this map.

Find:

- the river. It is called the River Tiber.

- the race track in the middle. Horses and chariots raced there.

- long thin buildings with lots of arches (there is one near the round end of the race track). They are called 'aqueducts'. The Romans built them to bring water to the city from the mountains far away. Some aqueducts were hundreds of kilometres long.

Julius Caesar and the Britons

This is a Roman general called Julius Caesar. The Romans sent him to conquer the people who lived in France. They called it Gaul.

While he was in Gaul, Caesar decided to cross the sea to find out what Britain was like. He landed in Kent.

Two thousand years ago the people who lived in Britain were called 'Celts' or 'Britons'. The Britons were farmers and fighters. They lived in large groups, or tribes. Each tribe had its own king.

This shield belonged to a wealthy Briton.

Archaeologists found this shield in the mud at the bottom of the River Thames at Battersea. It is made of bronze which is a mixture of copper and tin. Look at the patterns on it. What clues about the Britons do you think things like this gave Julius Caesar?

Archaeologist

Someone who finds out about the past from clues buried under the ground.

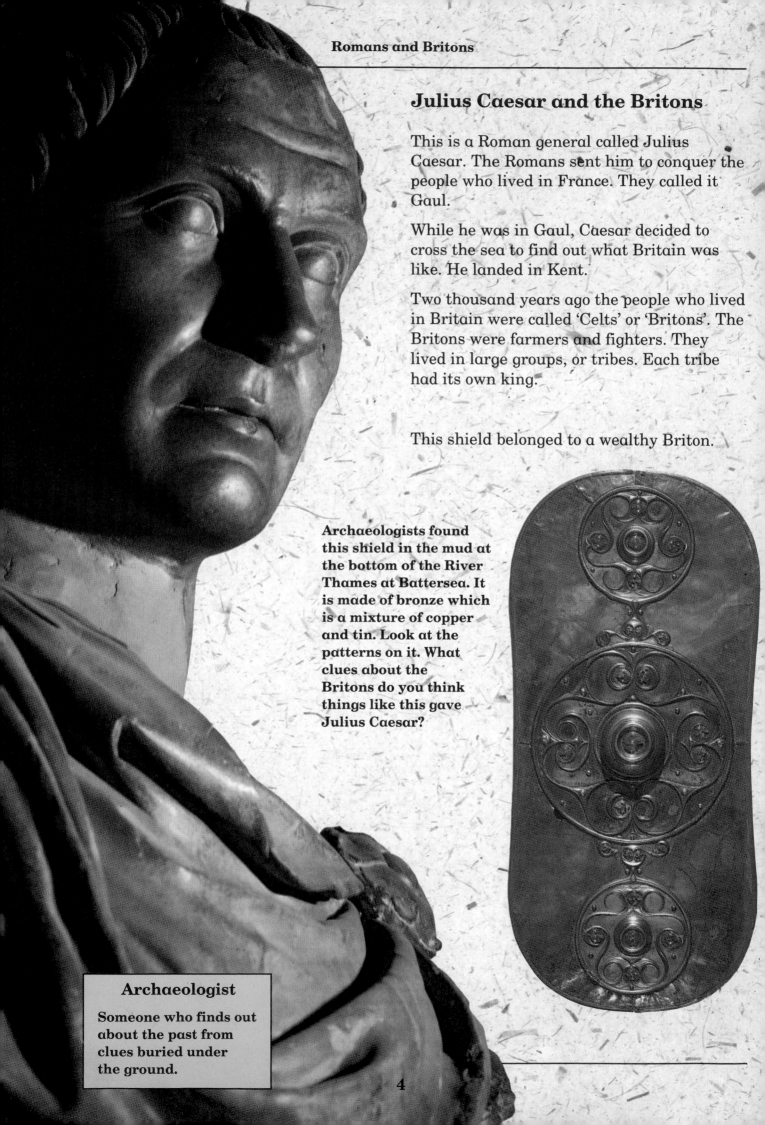

Most Britons could not afford such expensive things. They had a few iron tools on their farms and they made their own clothes from the wool of their sheep.

They used tools like these made from bone to make their clothes.

Find:

- the bone needles for sewing leather or cloth.

- the bone combs for combing wool from sheep to make clothes. Look at the patterns on them.

Julius Caesar decided that Britain was a rich country, it had tin, iron and copper and the people grew good crops, but he needed more soldiers to conquer it. He stayed for three weeks, then he went back to Gaul.

A year later he came back but this time he stayed for twelve weeks. The Roman army defeated the Britons but they were fierce fighters and would not give in.

Caesar decided it would be too difficult to conquer Britain. So he went away again.

The Romans invade Britain

The Romans left Britain alone for nearly a hundred years. Then the Emperor Claudius decided to make the Roman Empire bigger. He ordered his army to invade Britain.

The men who fought in the Roman army were paid to be full-time soldiers. The army was divided up into 'legions'. There were nearly five thousand men in a legion. They were called 'legionaries'.

This model of a Roman legionary is in The Yorkshire Museum. Find his:

- **shield, spear, sword and dagger.**

- **body armour. It is made of thin strips of steel fitted together with hooks and hinges. Why do you think it was made in strips like this?**

- **helmet. Why do you think the pieces covering his cheeks were on hinges? Why do you think there is a piece sticking out at the back?**

Here is the Roman Army on the march, crossing a bridge made of boats. The legionaries had to carry everything they needed with them.

Each legionary had to carry:
- **his weapons**
- **food for three days**
- **cooking pots**
- **an axe**
- **a hammer**
- **a bag of nails**
- **rope**
- **a cloak which was also his blanket**

Which of these can you see in the picture? How are they carried?

The Britons fought with swords and spears. They had slings for throwing stones. They did not wear armour. Most of them fought on foot, but some had horses, and the wealthiest had chariots.

Archaeologists made this model of a British war-chariot. They found some bits of chariots and used them as clues. How many horses were needed to pull it?

The Britons were clever at riding up to the enemy in their chariots, throwing their spears and then riding away before they could be attacked themselves.

An artist painted this picture to show how the Britons used war-chariots to fight the Romans. He used the descriptions of Roman writers as clues.

Drawing by Alan Sorrell

The Britons were used to fighting. Their kings often fought against each other. They built big forts on the tops of hills where families and animals could go for safety if a rival tribe invaded their land.

This is a hill-fort in Dorset, called Maiden Castle. Find:

- **the big space in the middle. This is where they built huts and kept animals.**

- **the four rings of earth walls and ditches to keep out attackers.**

- **the entrance. Why do you think it has so many twists and turns?**

When the Romans invaded the Britons in their hill-forts they had machines like catapults that could shoot round stones or short, heavy arrows called 'bolts'.

Here is the bolt that killed one of the Britons who tried to defend Maiden Castle against the Romans.

Find the bolt. It entered the Briton's body from the front and stuck in his spine. Archaeologists found the bones of hundreds more dead Britons at Maiden Castle. They had all been killed by the Romans.

It took the Romans four years to take over the south and east of Britain. After that they still had to fight the tribes in Wales and the north.

Some British kings welcomed the Romans. They agreed to obey them and to pay money to Rome. In return the Romans also called them 'kings' and allowed them to go on being in charge of their tribes.

Boudicca was the queen of one of these tribes. Nearly twenty years after the invasion the Romans insulted her. So she led her people to the Roman city of Colchester in Essex and they burnt it down. They even tried to smash this stone which some Romans had put up over the grave of a dead soldier. That is why his face is missing.

Next they destroyed London. Then a Roman army defeated them and Boudicca poisoned herself. You can find out more about her rebellion in the book called *Invasions*!.

Roman gravestones can give us clues about the Romans and the Britons. This soldier fought on horseback. Find:

- the frightened Briton underneath the horse. What do you think the Britons thought when they saw this? What clues does it give you about what Britons may have looked like?

- the writing. It is in Latin, the Romans' language. It says that the soldier's name was LONGINUS SDLAPEZE. Longinus was a Roman name. Sdlapeze was a name used by people from Thrace, which is now called Bulgaria. This is where he came from. People from all over the empire could serve in the Roman army.

Roads, Frontiers and Forts

Roads

The Romans built roads so that their army could march quickly from one part of the country to another. They built them as straight as possible so as to be able to take the shortest route. Many of our roads today still follow the line of Roman roads.

This is the Fosse Way. The Romans built it between Exeter and Lincoln. It has been used as a road ever since.

It was a big job to build a road.

First the army builders cleared the ground of rocks and trees.

Then they dug a trench where the road was to go and filled it with big stones.

Next they put in broken stones, pebbles, cement and sand which they packed down to make a firm base.

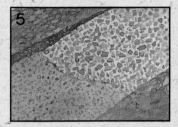

Then they added another layer of cement mixed with broken tiles.

On top of that they put paving stones to make the surface of the road.

They cut them so that they fitted together tightly.

They put stones called 'kerb stones' along the sides to hold in the paving stones and to make a channel for the water to run away.

This is what is left of a Roman road in North Yorkshire.
Find:

- the shaped paving stones.

The Imperial Post used covered coaches pulled by horses. Find the special badge on the side of the coach.

The roads were also used by a special postal service called the 'Imperial Post'. Important Romans could send messages and letters this way as long as they had the Emperor's permission.

On the Frontier

This is Hadrian's Wall. The Emperor Hadrian ordered the Romans to build it across the north of England. It is seventy-three miles long (one hundred and seventeen kilometres).

For three hundred years this wall was the 'frontier' of Roman Britain. That means it marked the end of the part of Britain that the Romans ruled and the beginning of the part they did not.

Find:

- the wall. It is four metres high, and wide enough to walk on. Why do you think the Romans built it to follow the top of the cliffs?

- the ditch with mounds of earth on each side. The Romans dug it on their side of the wall. Roman soldiers were the only people allowed to be in the space between the ditch and the wall.

The Romans called all the people who lived outside the frontiers of the Empire '**barbarians**', which meant foreigners. The barbarians on the far side of Hadrian's Wall lived in what is now Scotland. What do you think they thought when they looked at the wall?

Most barbarians were glad they did not have to obey the Romans, but they often wanted to cross the frontier to buy and sell things. The Romans let them through as long as they did not carry weapons. Roman soldiers had to go with them.

It took six years to build Hadrian's Wall. Roman soldiers were good at building walls and forts. A Roman artist carved this picture to show how they did it.

Barbarians

From the Latin word 'Barbarus' which meant strange, foreign or uncivilised.

Look for the different jobs the soldiers are doing. Find them:

- **digging ditches.**
- **taking away the earth in baskets.**
- **cutting wood and hammering it into the ground.**
- **building the wall.**

Find the shield, spear and helmet.

Who do you think is in charge? How can you tell?

The soldiers who guarded Hadrian's Wall lived in forts. You can still visit some of the forts today. This photograph shows what is left of the fort at Housesteads. It was taken from an aeroplane so you can see the shape of the fort.

Roman doctors used instruments like these to do operations in the hospital. Alcohol was the only pain-killer they had to give their patients. What kind of operations do you think they had to do?

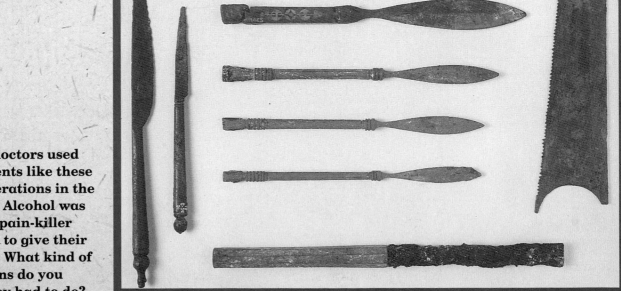

This model shows how the fort at Housesteads looked in Roman times.

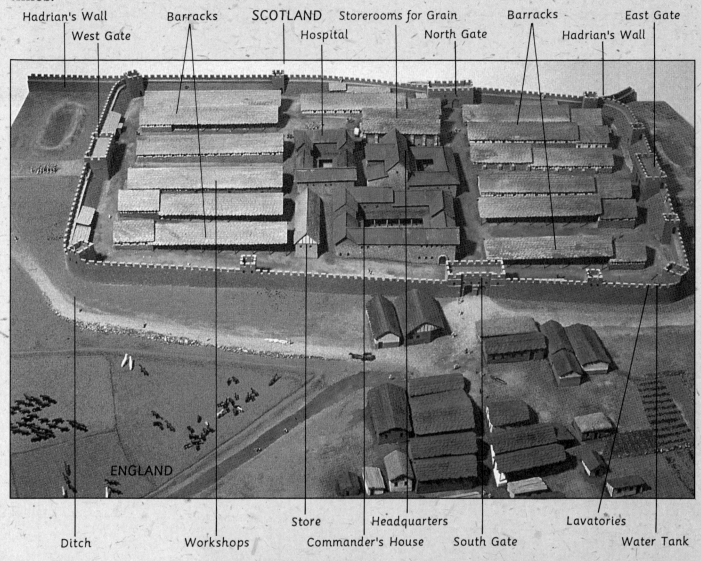

Hadrian's Wall
West Gate
Barracks
SCOTLAND
Hospital
Storerooms for Grain
North Gate
Barracks
East Gate
Hadrian's Wall
ENGLAND
Ditch
Workshops
Store
Commander's House
Headquarters
South Gate
Lavatories
Water Tank

Look again at the photograph of the fort. Use this model to work out which parts of the fort are still there today.

The soldiers at Housesteads played games in their spare time.
Find:

- **the board**
- **counters**
- **dice**

The People and their Homes

People, Clothes and Jewellery

A Roman soldier called Caius Augustinus had this carving made in memory of his dead wife and children. He put it over their grave. You can see it today in a museum in York.

The writing on the stone says Caius Augustinus set it up in memory of his 'darling wife' who lived 39 years 7 months 11 days, his son who lived 1 year 3 days and his daughter who lived 1 year 9 months 5 days.

Caius's wife was called Flavia Augustina. You can see her on the left. Caius himself is shown beside her, with the children in front.

The carving shows the sort of clothes worn by a rich Roman family.

Flavia is wearing a long tunic which comes down to her ankles and a cloak thrown back over her shoulders. Caius is wearing a shorter tunic with a hooded cloak over it. The children are dressed like their parents.

Men and women wore shirts under their tunics and a piece of cloth wrapped round and tied at the waist instead of pants. Women used a strip of cloth as a bra.

Roman underwear probably looked like this. This girl may be a dancer or an acrobat.

Flavia and her family wore sandals and shoes made of leather like these. Out of doors they wore boots.

When the Romans defeated a barbarian tribe they usually captured some of its people and kept them as **slaves**.

Most rich Roman families owned slaves who did the cooking and shopping and worked in the house.

Look at the men in this shop. The two men sitting down are buying cloth. The two standing beside them are their slaves. What is the difference between the clothes of the slaves and of their owners?

The owners of the slaves are wearing something called a 'toga'. It was a long white robe made of wool. Only free men were allowed to wear it, and they usually wore it on important occasions. Even so, most free men in Britain preferred to wear a tunic.

Slaves

People who had to work for other people without having any wages. They could be sold by their owners to someone else.

Here is another gravestone that tells us about the people in Roman Britain and what they were like. The writing says that it was put up by a man called Barates in memory of his wife. He was a free man who came from Syria, a far away part of the Empire.

Barates bought a British slave girl called Regina. Later on he freed her and they got married. Regina is a Latin word that means 'queen.' We do not know who gave Regina her name. Perhaps it was Barates himself.

The carving of Regina shows some of her things. Find:

- **her gown. Is it a nice one? How can you tell?**

- **the jewel box in her hand.**

- **her work basket with wool in it.**

Perhaps Regina had a dressing table like this.

All these things (except the flowers!) come from the time of the Romans and were found in Britain. Find:

- the bottles for make-up and perfume.
- the hairpins made of bone.
- the lamp. Lamps like this were made in Italy and were brought to Britain by boat.
- the bead necklaces.
- the bronze mirror.
- the ring. Men and women wore rings.
- the nail cleaners.

Perhaps she wore jewellery like this.

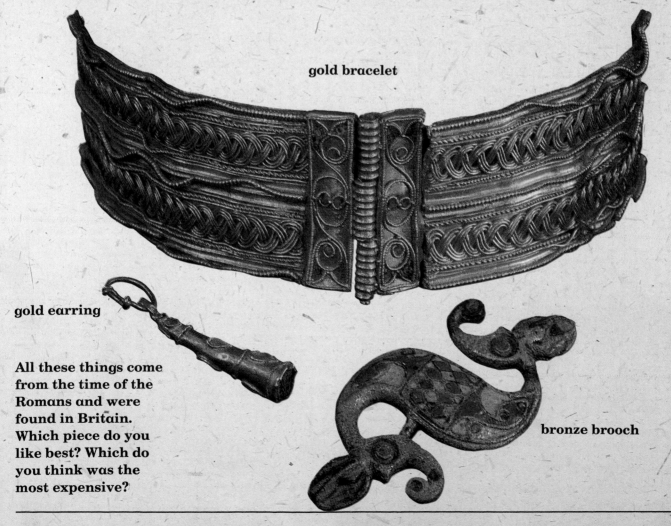

gold bracelet

gold earring

bronze brooch

All these things come from the time of the Romans and were found in Britain. Which piece do you like best? Which do you think was the most expensive?

Growing Up and Going to School

This carving shows a Roman boy growing up.

1 The boy is fed by his mother.
2 His father takes him in his arms.
3 He learns to drive a goat cart.
4 He goes to school.

Roman girls and boys stayed at home until they were seven. They played with toys like these.

These toys were found in Britain. What is the same about the toys children play with today? What is different?

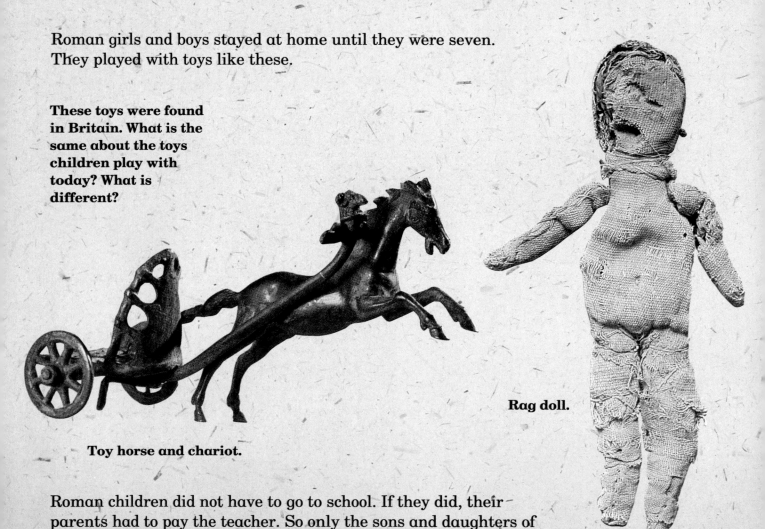

Rag doll.

Toy horse and chariot.

Roman children did not have to go to school. If they did, their parents had to pay the teacher. So only the sons and daughters of wealthy families went to school. They started when they were seven.

They learnt to read and write and count. The Romans wrote their numbers like this:

I II III IV V VI VII VIII IX X
1 2 3 4 5 6 7 8 9 10

Four (IV) is one less than five (V).
Seven (VII) is two more than five (V).

How do you think they wrote fifteen?

There was no '0' in Roman numbers. They wrote other numbers like this:

L C D M
50 100 500 1000

Older boys studied Latin and Greek as well as some History, Geography and **Astronomy** and how to make speeches.

Girls left school before boys. Even so, some of them studied Latin, Greek and Music.

Astronomy

The study of the Sun, Moon and stars.

At school.
Find:

- the master.

- the boy reading to him from a roll of paper. This was made from papyrus reeds which were pressed together and dried.

- the boy who has come late. He is carrying a bag.

Many of the children who did not go to school probably learnt to read, write and count from their parents. Mothers taught girls to spin and weave. Fathers taught boys to fight with swords and ride horses.

At Home

The Britons lived in round houses with one room for the whole family. They built them with wood, straw and mud.

The Romans knew how to build houses using wood and stone with tiles for the roof. They were usually on one level like a bungalow. The smaller ones had two or three rooms but rich people lived in big houses with lots of rooms round a courtyard, these houses even had central heating.

Here are the remains of a room in one of those houses.

Find:

- **the walls. What are they made of?**

- **the floor. It is covered with tiny pieces of coloured tile made into a pattern. This is called a 'mosaic'.**

- **the piles of tiles for holding up the floor. A fire heated the air in the space under the floor which warmed up the room.**

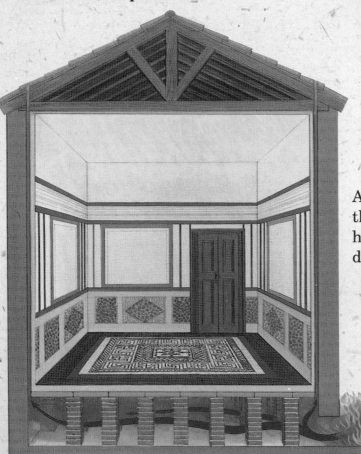

Archaeologists use clues from remains like this to work out how the Romans built their houses and what they looked like. This drawing shows you what they think.

Find:

- **the fire to heat the air.**

- **the hollow walls. The hot air in the walls heated the sides of the room as well as the floor.**

This room has been built in the Museum of London to show what the dining room in a Roman house looked like.

The Romans used glass bottles and cups like these in the dining room. They came to Britain from Gaul and Germany.

Find:

- the couch. The Romans often lay on their sides and ate from a table beside it. It was also used as a bed.

- the cupboard. All the pots and vases come from Roman times and were found in Britain.

- the walls. They were covered in plaster and then decorated.

This room has been built in the Museum of London to show what the kitchen in a Roman house looked like.

Drawing by Alan Sorrell

Find:

- the metal pot on the stove. It is standing on an iron grid. It was heated by a charcoal fire in the square hole underneath it. Charcoal is made from partly burnt wood.

- the charcoal stored under the fire-place.

- the tall jars with pointed ends. These held olive oil or wine or sea-food. The smaller pointed jar held dried fruit. All these things came from different parts of the empire.

- the bronze saucepans.

- the mixing bowls with wide rims on the table underneath. They were used to grind things into very tiny pieces.

Here are some of the things that the Romans liked to eat.

They were very interested in food. They liked fish and shell-fish such as oysters, cockles and mussels. Also meat of all kinds and birds such as pigeons, pheasants, chickens and geese.

For a treat they liked snails and dormice which they fattened up specially.

They used a lot of spices in their cooking, and herbs such as mint, parsley, bayleaves and thyme. They also liked a strong fish sauce made from anchovies.

They cooked with olive oil and they sweetened their food with honey. They drank wine.

The Romans also liked fruit and vegetables. Apples, some grapes, peas and beans already grew in Britain. The Romans introduced new vegetables such as cabbages, onions, leeks, carrots, cucumbers, marrows, parsnips, turnips and celery. They brought in lentils and dried fruit which were grown in other parts of the Empire.

How many of these things can you find in the pictures on these two pages?

Life and Work in Roman Britain

Town Life

The Britons did not live in towns. Before the Romans came, the nearest thing to a town was a big hill-fort like Maiden Castle. The Romans built many big new towns. They called this one 'Verulamium'. Today it is called St. Albans.

Drawing by Alan Sorrell

Find:

- the town walls.

- the gates. How many are there?

- the streets. They are all straight and divide the town into blocks. The Romans always planned their towns like this.

Look near the centre of the town. Find the open square with the big building down one side. Archaeologists found these writing things where that building stood in Roman times. They are clues to what it was for.

It was the place where the people who ran the town worked. They had to do a lot of writing. It was also the law courts. The Romans called it the 'basilica'.

Find:

- the wooden boards tied together. They were covered with soft beeswax.

- the two pens. People used the sharp end of the pen to write in the wax. They used the flat end to smooth out mistakes.

- the inkwell. Sometimes they used a pen and ink to write onto parchment. Parchment is made from the skin of sheep.

- the oil lamp, beeswax and seals. When the letter had been written the boards were closed and tied with string. The wax was melted over the lamp and a blob of hot wax dropped on the knot. Then the seal was pressed into the wax. Why do you think they did this? After the letter had been sent and read, the boards were warmed to melt the wax. Then they could be used again.

Drawing by Alan Sorrell

The Romans called the big square in front of the basilica, the 'forum'. There were shops and stalls all round it. It was the main meeting place in the town. The forum at Verulamium looked something like this.

An artist used the clues found by archaeologists to paint this. What different things are people doing in the forum?

The shops looked like this one.

Find:

- the customer with her shopping list.

- the shopkeeper. What does he sell? What is he doing?
- the scales for weighing the goods.

These were found in York. The thing at the top is called a 'steelyard'. It was used for weighing goods.

The coins are made of silver. They always showed the head of the Emperor on one side. Roman soldiers were paid with coins. Perhaps a soldier spent these in the forum at York.

The steelyard is made of bronze. Look again at the scales in the shop. How is it the same as them? How is it different? How do you think it worked?

Here is another stall from the forum. It belongs to someone who makes knives.

Archaeologists built this stall using some of the things they found from Roman London. How many different kinds of knife can you see? Why do you think there are so many different shapes? What other things can you see on display?

29

This is one of the baths in the Roman town of Bath. It was a warm bath meant for swimming. There were other smaller baths and heated rooms round the sides. How is this the same as a swimming pool today? Is anything different?

Every Roman town had public baths with an outdoor courtyard for exercise. The Romans liked to go there every day to get clean, to keep fit and to meet each other and chat.

There were several rooms in the public baths. First you undressed in the changing room. Then you exercised in the courtyard. Next you sat in a room heated with warm air. Then you went to a very hot one.

The hot air made you sweat so now you went to an attendant who rubbed you over with olive oil and then scraped it off with a special tool called a 'strigil'.

Next you sat or swam in a warm bath before finishing off with a dip in a very cold bath.

A strigil and oil bottle found in the Roman baths in London. Why do you think the strigil is shaped like this?

Many Roman towns had a theatre. People went there to watch plays. They also liked to see bear-baiting, wrestling and fights to the death between armed men called gladiators.

Drawing by Alan Sorrell

This is how the theatre at Verulamium may have looked. The artist used clues found by archaeologists to paint this. Find:

- the wooden seats for the audience. More than five thousand people could sit there. How did they fit in so many?

- the entrances for the audience. How did they get to their seats?

- the stage for the actors. Their dressing rooms were behind it.

- the space in front of the stage. This was where the fighting and bear-baiting happened. When there was a play on, extra seats were put in there for important people.

Country Life

This model shows a small farm belonging to Britons in the north of England at the time of the Romans.

Find:

- **the round houses with thatched roofs.**
- **the stone walls.**
- **the ditch round the outside.**

The people who lived here kept cows and sheep and grew crops of wheat, oats and barley on the land around their farm.

Here is a farmer ploughing a field so that he can sow seeds for crops in it.

This statue was found in the north of England, it was made out of bronze in Roman times. Find:

- **the farmer.**
- **the plough.**
- **the oxen pulling the plough.**

Drawing by Alan Sorrell

The Romans built houses in the countryside as well as in towns. They called their country houses 'villas'. Villas were farms as well as houses. The Britons living nearby had to help the owner with the farming. He sold the meat, corn and fruit from his farm to people living in the nearest town.

This villa was at Lullingstone in Kent.

- **How is it different to the Britons' farms? Is anything the same?**

- **What do you think the Britons who lived nearby thought when they saw it being built?**

- **Do you think the owner was rich? How can you tell?**

This mosaic was on the floor of the main room in Lullingstone villa. What clues does it give you about what the villa was like inside? Find:

- **the patterns. How many can you see?**

- **the pictures. What can you see in them?**

Trade with the Empire

The Romans were used to a comfortable life. They liked to be able to buy things from all over the Empire.

Here are some of the things that were taken from Britain to other parts of the Empire.

This is a model of the sort of boat that came to Britain. You can see it in the Museum of London. Find:

* the masts and sails. How many are there?
* the anchor.
* the little boat beside it. What is it doing?
* the gang-plank over to the quay. What are the sailors unloading?

So boats like this came to British ports, such as London and York, full of goods from far away places. They sailed away loaded with things from Britain.

Animal skins.

Hunting dogs.

Corn.

Pearls and oysters.

Gold, silver and lead.

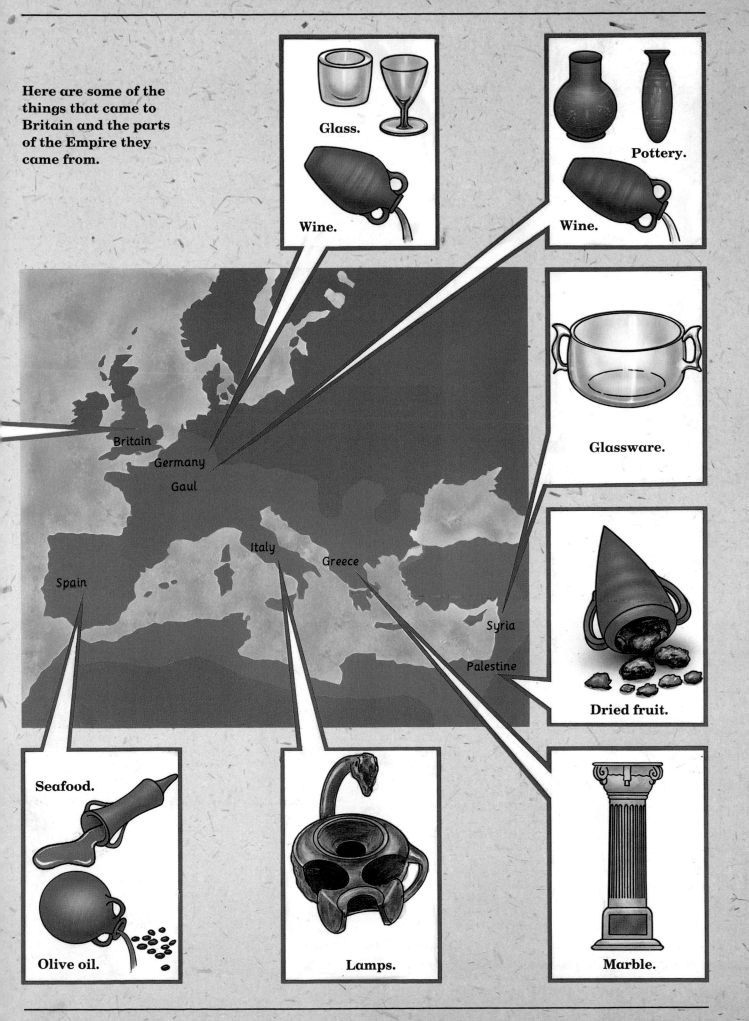

Here are some of the things that came to Britain and the parts of the Empire they came from.

Glass.

Wine.

Pottery.

Wine.

Glassware.

Dried fruit.

Britain

Germany

Gaul

Italy

Greece

Syria

Palestine

Spain

Seafood.

Olive oil.

Lamps.

Marble.

Religious Life

Roman and British gods

The Romans kept a little statue like this on a shelf in the hall of the house.

It was the god that looked after the house and all the people in it. They called it a 'Lar'.

Every day the head of the household went to the statue of the Lar and put food and wine in front of it as a gift to the god.

This statue of a Lar was found in Norfolk. It is nine centimetres high.

The Romans had many gods. Each god was in charge of a different thing. They thought it was very important to give presents to the gods so that the gods would look after them and help them.

When they thought a god had helped them, the Romans often gave the god a 'thank you' present. Someone gave the god in charge of medicine this little model of a leg.

It was to say 'thank you' because a broken leg had got better.

The Britons already had their own gods such as these three Mother Goddesses.

The Mother Goddesses are holding trays. Two have food on them, one has loaves of bread. Which is which? Look at their clothes and hair. Do you think these are clues to how British women looked?

The Romans hoped the Britons would start to worship Roman gods. Some did but many carried on as before.

The Romans' chief gods were Jupiter, the
king of the gods, and Juno, the queen.
Jupiter was also the god of the sky and
weather. Juno was the goddess who looked
after women.

This is Mars. He was the god of war so he
was very popular with soldiers.

**Three men called
Colasuni, Bruccius
and Caratius had this
statue made to give to
Mars. Find their
names on the base.
It was found in
Lincolnshire.**

This statue is Minerva. She was the goddess
of science and of making things.
Archaeologists have found a lot of statues
like this one in Britain.

The Romans also borrowed gods from other parts of the world. This is a carving of a Persian god called Mithras. It was found in York. Roman soldiers liked to worship him.

The story of Mithras said that he killed a wild bull and from the blood of the bull came all life on earth. Find:

- **Mithras.**
- **the bull.**

What is Mithras holding in his hand? What is he doing?

The Romans also said that their Emperor was a god. When they first settled in Britain, they built a temple in Colchester for the worship of the Emperor Claudius.

This is the head of a statue of Claudius. It may have come from the temple.

The Romans ordered everyone in the Empire to worship the Emperor and Jupiter, the king of the gods. If they obeyed they were allowed to worship other gods as well.

Christianity

More than two hundred and fifty years after the Romans took over
Britain, the Emperor Constantine changed the Roman religion.
He said that everyone in the Empire had to worship the Christian
God. That meant they had to believe in the life and teaching of
Jesus Christ.

This mosaic comes from the floor of a villa in Dorset. It shows
the picture of a man who may be
Jesus Christ.

Find the sign behind the man's head. It shows the first three letters of the name 'Christ' in Greek.

It must have taken
a long time for people to stop
worshipping their old gods, even though the
Emperor told them to. Many of them pretended to worship
the Christian God and went on worshipping their old gods secretly.

These pictures are clues that some people did become Christian.

Archaeologists found these things in the grave of a dead woman who died in Roman times. Her family put some of her jewellery in the grave with her dead body. The Latin writing carved in bone says:

'Hail sister may you live with God.'

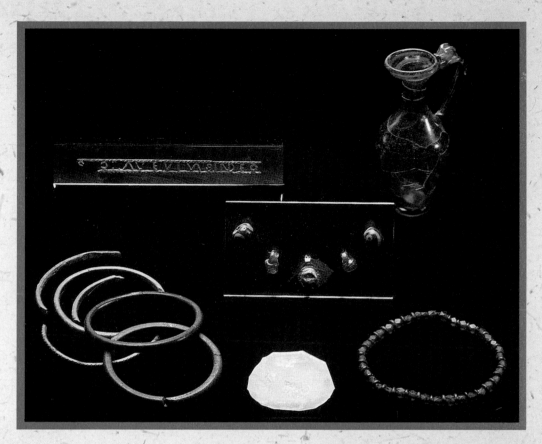

These things were found nearly twenty years ago in a place where there was once a Roman town. They are all made of silver and were made in Roman times. The writing on them shows that Christians used them in their church services.

What Did the Romans Leave Behind?

Why the Romans left Britain

The Romans built this fort about two hundred and fifty years after they first settled in Britain.

Pirates were starting to attack villas and villages near the sea. They landed on the beach, stole food and gold and silver, then sailed away again.

Roman soldiers were sent to forts like this to try to keep the pirates out.

The pirates were Saxons. They sailed across the North Sea from Germany to raid Britain.

They were not the only people to raid the Empire. Many barbarian tribes now wanted to live inside its frontiers because there seemed to be plenty of land and the people were rich.

The Romans did not want to let them in, so the tribes attacked them.

Barbarian Tribes

Britain

Germany

Gaul

Italy

Greece

North Africa

Syria

In the end the Emperor decided he needed the Roman army in Britain to go to other parts of the Empire to defend it against the tribes.

By now the Britons were used to being part of the Empire. They begged the Emperor to send soldiers to defend them against the Picts, Scots and Saxons who were attacking Britain. But the Emperor said they would have to look after themselves.

This is where the different tribes attacked the frontiers of the Roman Empire.

Words, Names and Places

You can still see some of the buildings the Romans left behind. This is what is left of the city wall they built round London. The white building which you can just see next to it is the Museum of London where you can see a lot of other Roman things.

Find out if there are any remains of Roman buildings near your home.

Find out if there is a museum where you can see some of the things that people used in Roman times.

Perhaps you live in or near one of the towns the Romans built, or near one of the roads they made.

These are the words written on the gravestone of a British woman called Regina who married a soldier in the Roman army.

Find the name REGINA on it. Regina is a Latin word that means queen. Now find the word LIBERTA next to it. 'Liberta' is a Latin word. Liberta means free.

There is an English word like it – liberty. It also means free. Our word liberty comes from the Latin word 'liberta'.

Find the word NATIONE at the end of the second line. Our word 'nation' comes from it. Nation means country.

Lots of English words come from Latin. That is because some people, especially Christian priests, went on speaking and writing Latin in Britain even after the Romans had left.

Some people have names that come from Latin words. For example, Lucy comes from the Latin word 'lux' meaning light. The Romans often called girls 'Lucia' and boys 'Lucius' if they were born at day-break.

Art and Buildings

This is a model of the temple that the Romans built at Colchester in honour of the Emperor Claudius. They copied this way of building from the Greeks.

This is the British Museum in London. It was built about a hundred and fifty years ago. The person who designed it copied the look of a Roman or Greek temple. What did they do to make it look the same?

See if any buildings near you copy this look.

An artist made this big silver dish in Roman times. It was found in Suffolk.

Why do you think artists today think Roman artists were very clever?

In the News

People are still finding things from Roman times.

In 1990 some workmen were digging a hole for a pipe near Cambridge.

They found these little figures made of clay.

They were buried with the dead body of a Roman child aged about eighteen months.

They were near a Roman road called Ermine Street which linked the south of England to the north. It went from London to York and on to Hadrian's Wall.